WELCOME THE S

Celebrate each season and holiday with these vibrant wall hangings!

LEISURE ARTS, INC. • Maumelle, Arkansas

WELCOME HOME

WELCOME GUESTS into your home with this charming wall hanging. Featuring interchangeable banners for each season, this design makes an inviting statement all year-round.

COLOR KEY: WELCOME HOME HOUSE

◆	Bright Yellow	➜	Lime Green
×	Dark Blue	♥	Red
⬮	Lavender	●	Rose
★	Light Blue	·	White
▼	Light Pink		

Backstitch Floss (4 strands)

- Dark Blue (wavy line)
- Dark Brown (solid line)

Overcast the edges using yarn that matches adjacent stitches.

Gray area indicates last row of previous section of design.

WELCOME HOME HOUSE
78 × 97 threads

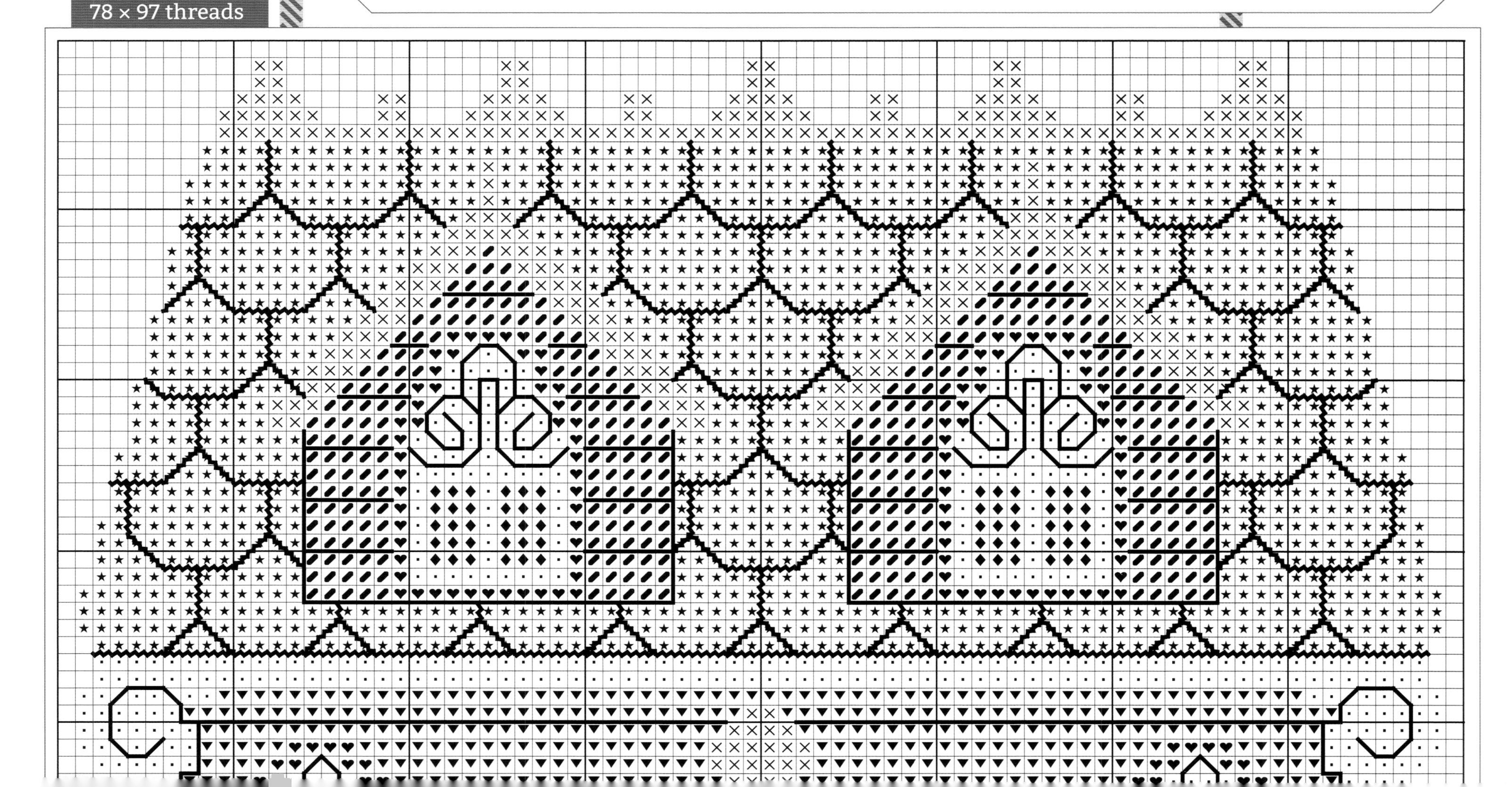

Plastic Canvas Size Needed: 13½" × 16½"

WELCOME HOME SPRING
71 × 21 threads

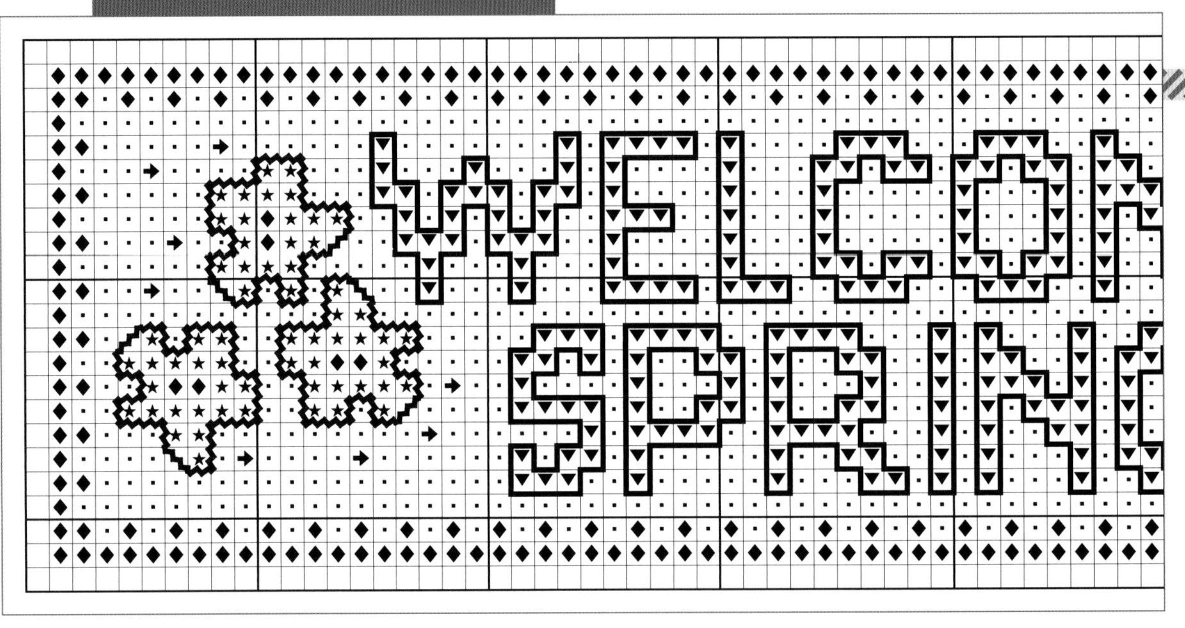

Plastic Canvas Size Needed: 13" × 5½"

WELCOME HOME SUMMER
71 × 21 threads

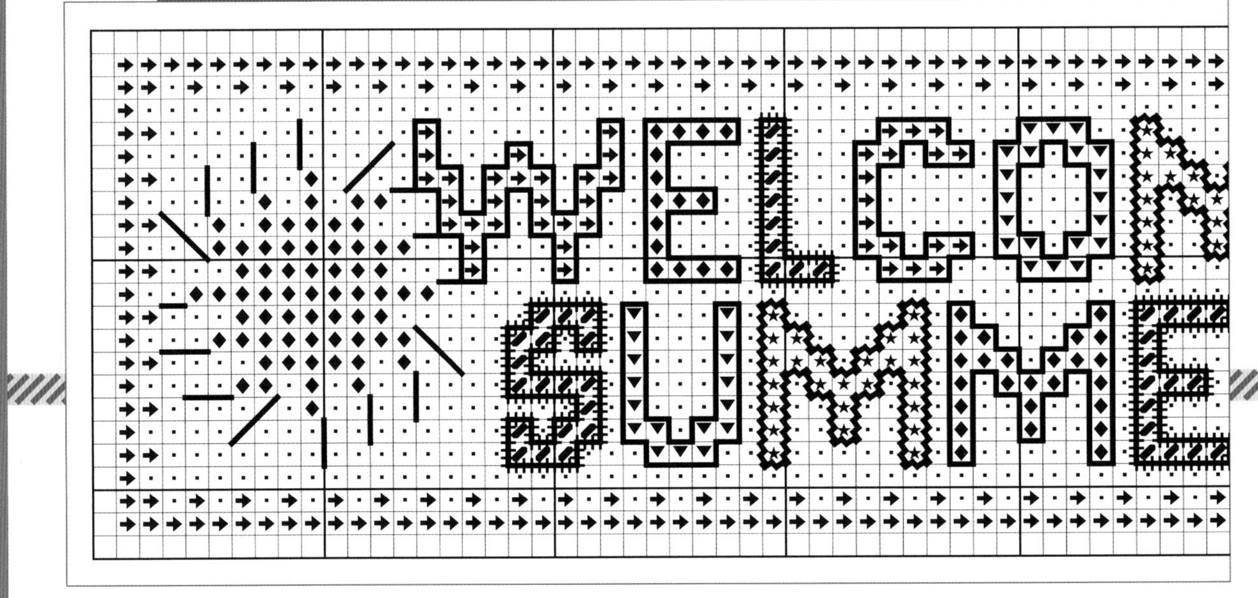

Plastic Canvas Size Needed: 13" × 5½"

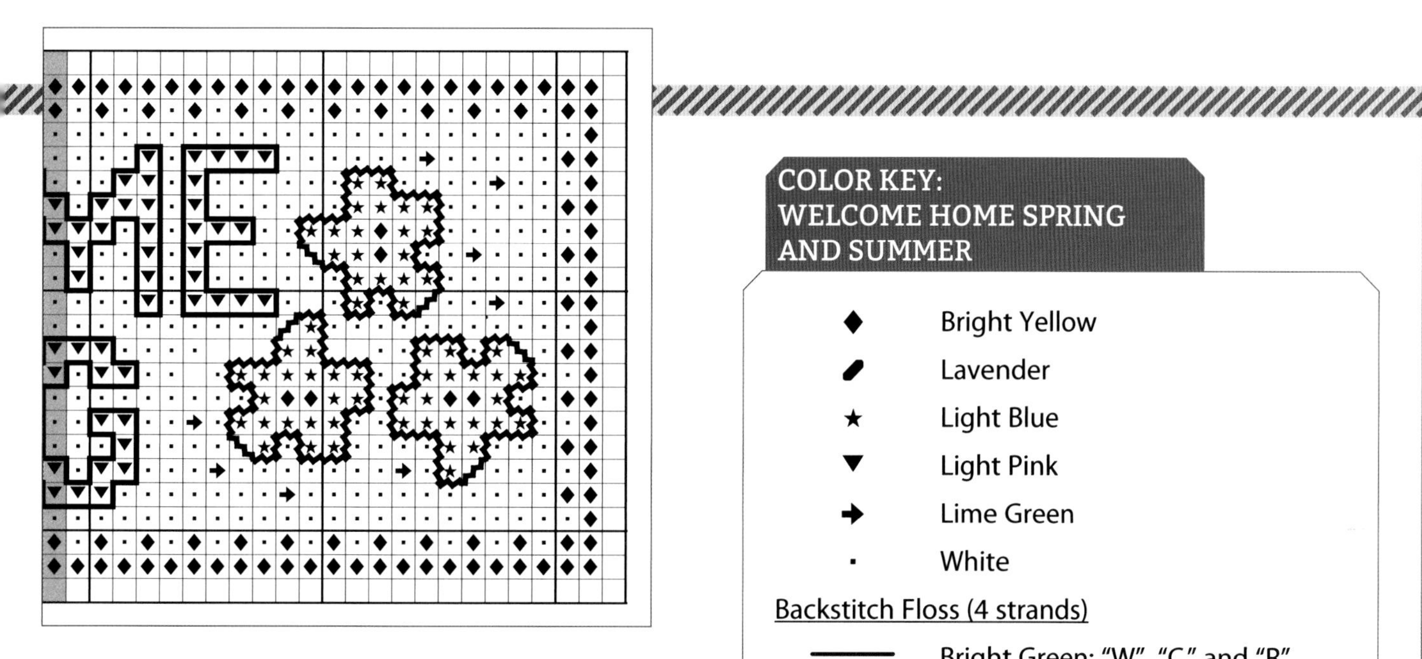

COLOR KEY: WELCOME HOME SPRING AND SUMMER

- ◆ Bright Yellow
- Lavender
- ★ Light Blue
- ▼ Light Pink
- ➔ Lime Green
- · White

Backstitch Floss (4 strands)

- Bright Green: "W", "C," and "R" outlines in WELCOME SUMMER
- Dark Blue
- Dark Straw: First "E" and second "M" outlines in WELCOME SUMMER
- Rose: outline around WELCOME SPRING and "O" and "U" outlines in WELCOME SUMMER
- Dark Violet
- Topaz: Sun rays in WELCOME SUMMER

Overcast the edges using yarn that matches adjacent stitches.

☐ Gray area indicates last row of previous section of design.

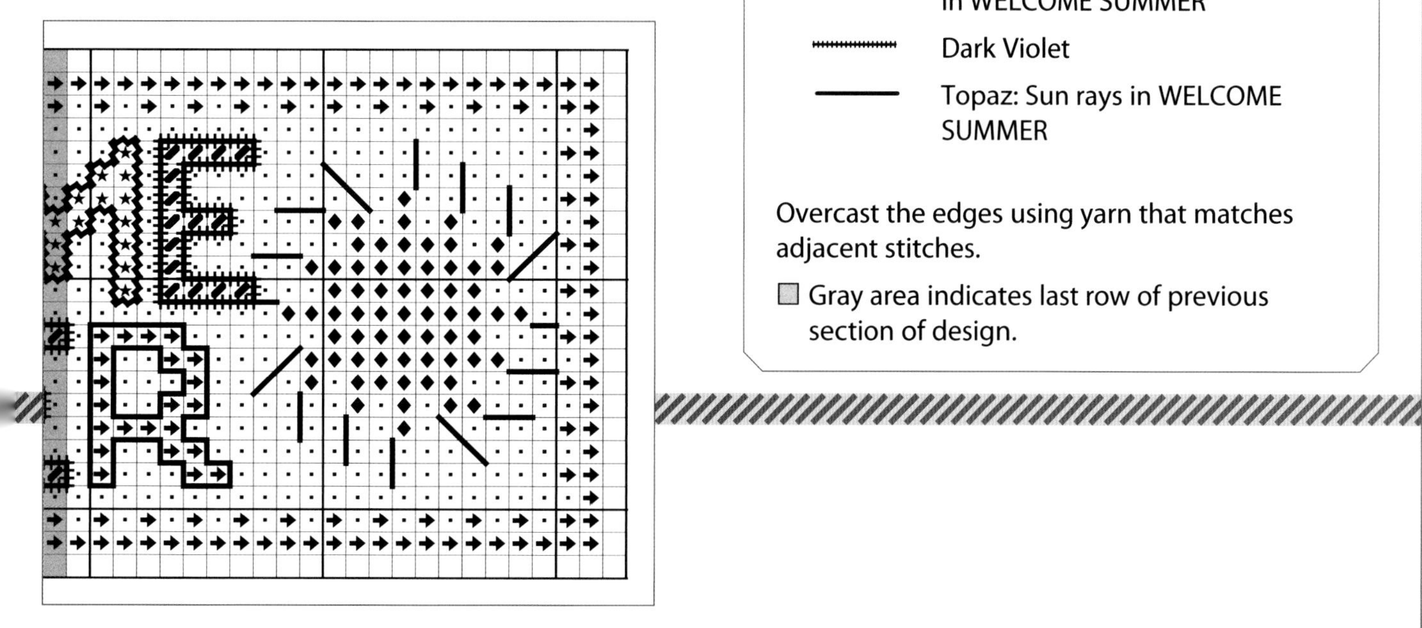

WELCOME HOME FALL
71 × 21 threads

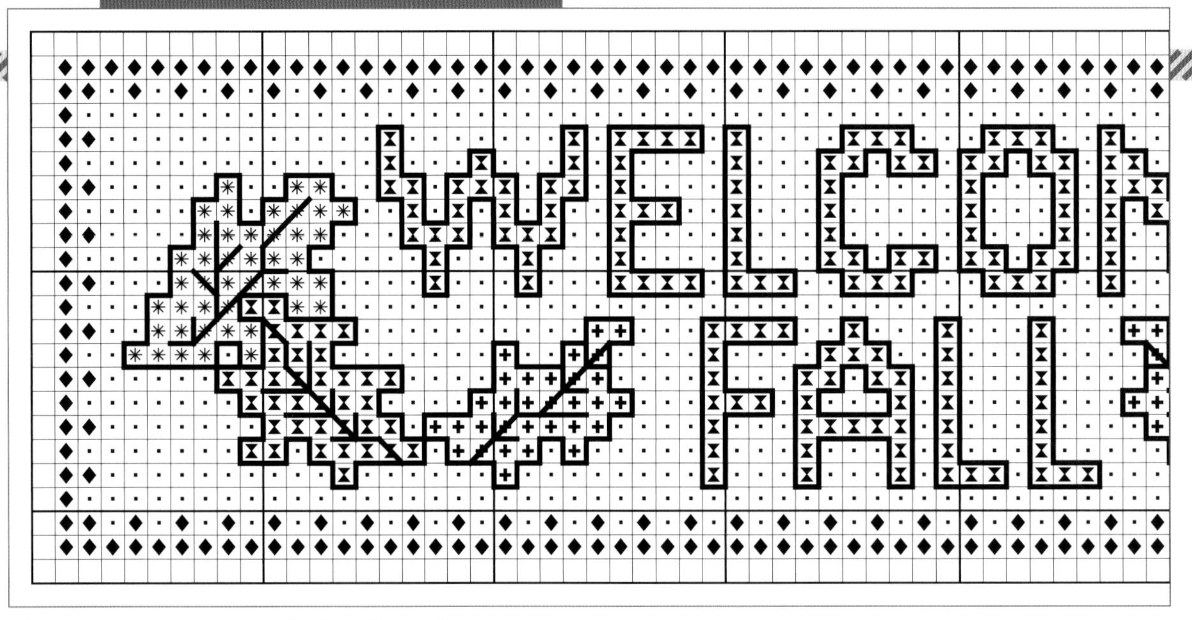

Plastic Canvas Size Needed: 13" × 5½"

WELCOME HOME WINTER
71 × 21 threads

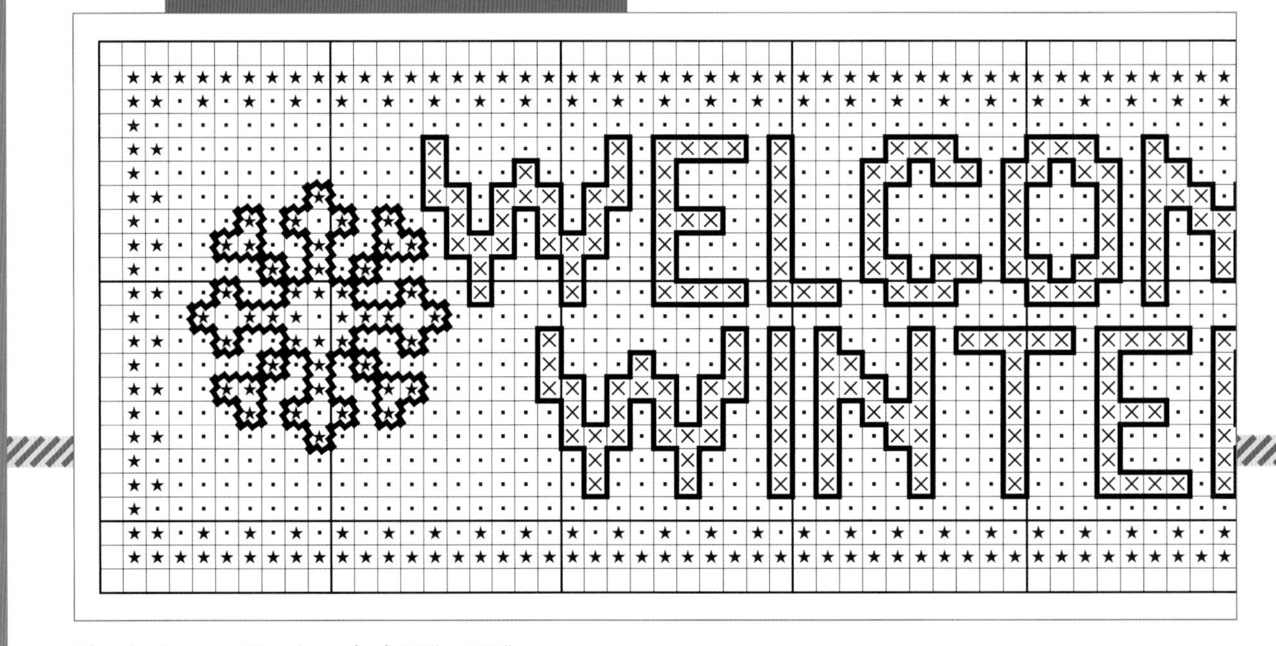

Plastic Canvas Size Needed: 13" × 5½"

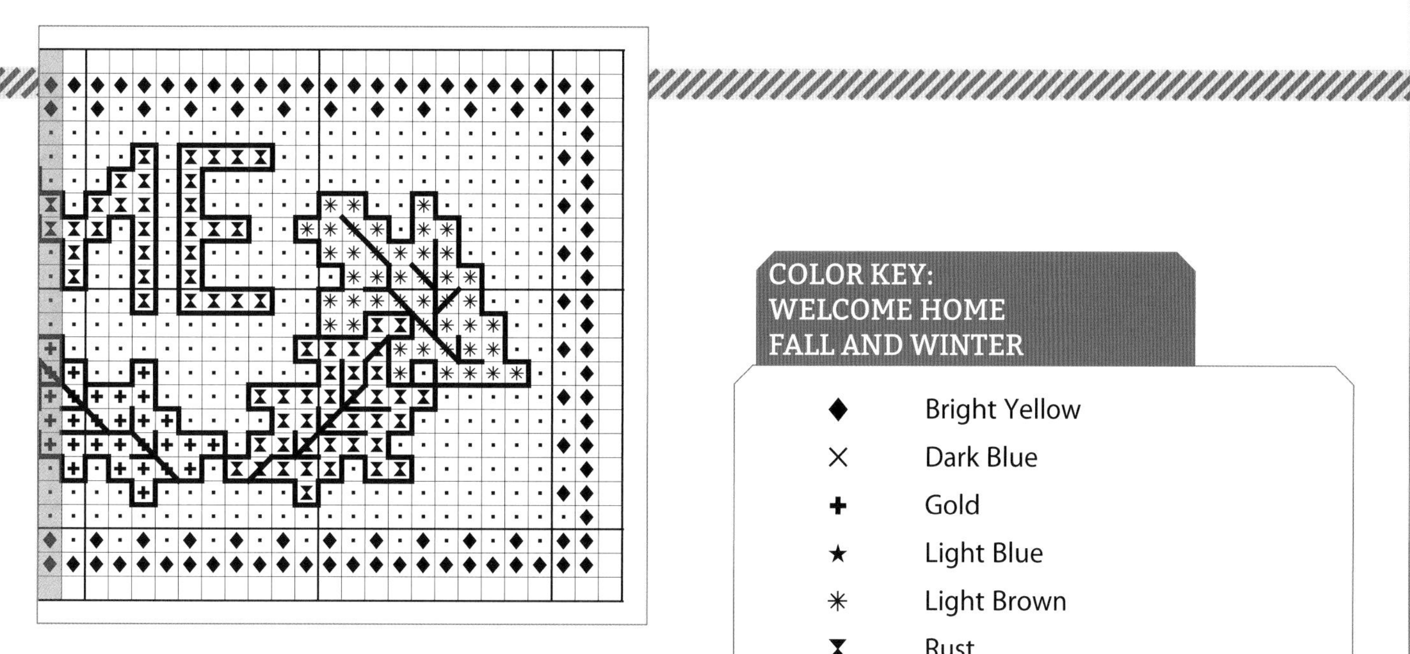

COLOR KEY: WELCOME HOME FALL AND WINTER

◆	Bright Yellow
×	Dark Blue
✚	Gold
★	Light Blue
✳	Light Brown
⧗	Rust
▪	White

Backstitch Floss (4 strands)

———	Black: outlines around WELCOME WINTER
~~	Dark Blue
———	Dark Brown: leaves and outlines around WELCOME FALL

Overcast the edges using yarn that matches adjacent stitches.

☐ Gray area indicates last row of previous section of design.

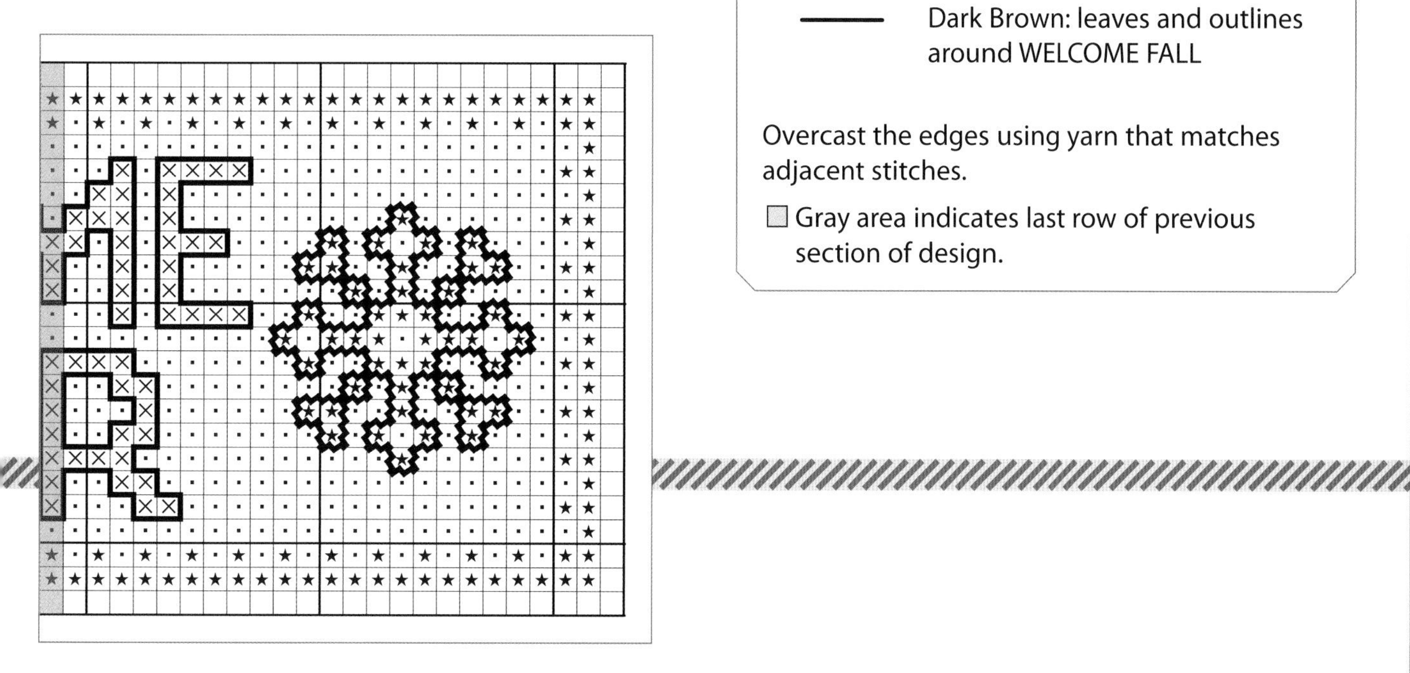

SEASONS OF WELCOME

CELEBRATE EVERY SEASON and every reason with this design! Featuring center inserts with fun holiday motifs, you'll be able to festively decorate your home for every occasion.

Be Mine
ABC

COLOR KEY: SEASONS OF WELCOME QUILT BLOCK

☆	Bright Yellow
◘	Dark Blue
×	Lavender
∀	Light Blue
♣	Medium Yellow Green
♡	Rose
·	White

Backstitch Floss (4 strands)

—— Black

Overcast the edges using yarn that matches adjacent stitches.

Gray area indicates last row of previous section of design.

Plastic Canvas Size Needed: 12½" × 15½"

SEASONS OF WELCOME QUILT BLOCK

69 × 89 threads

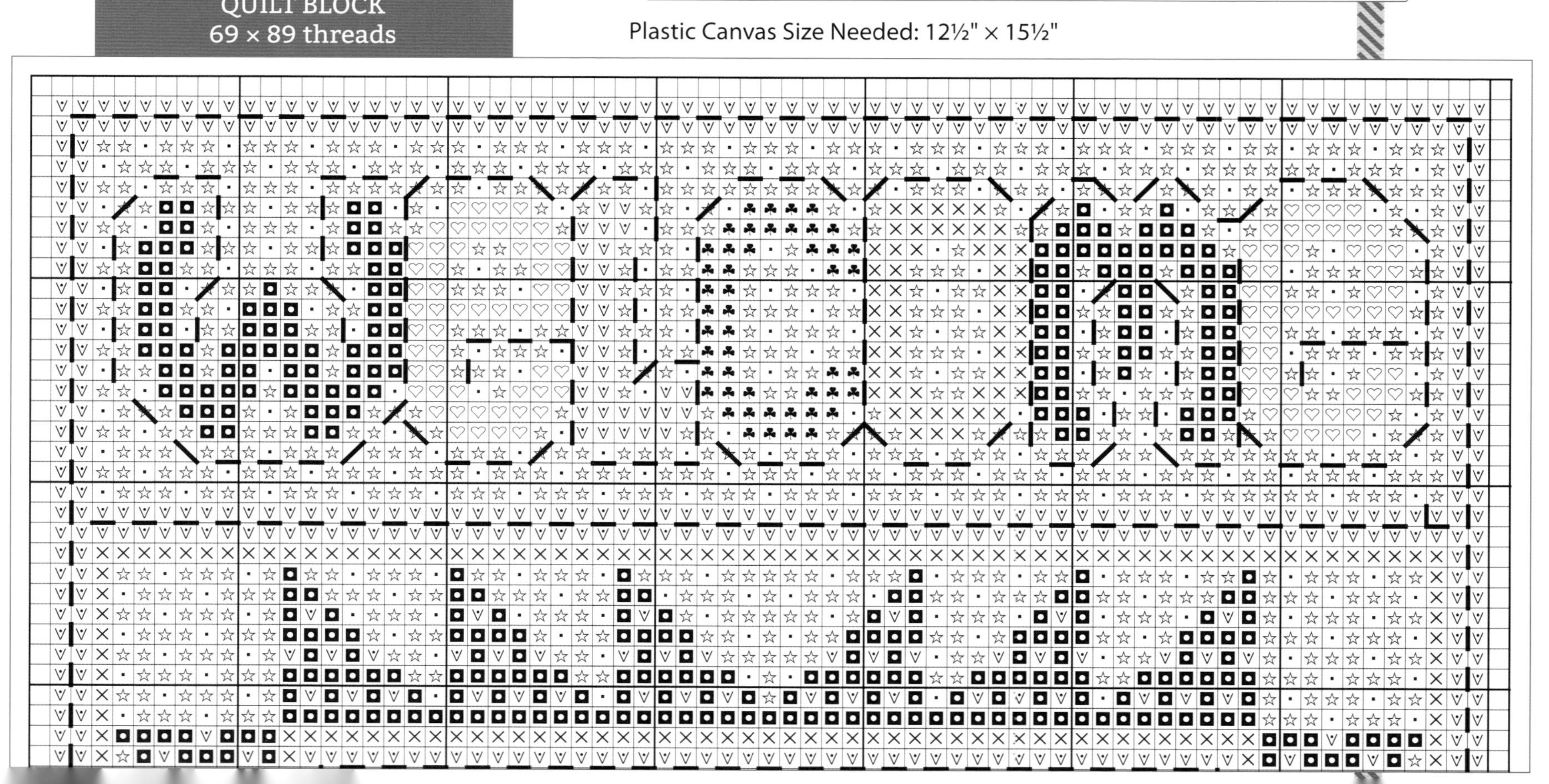

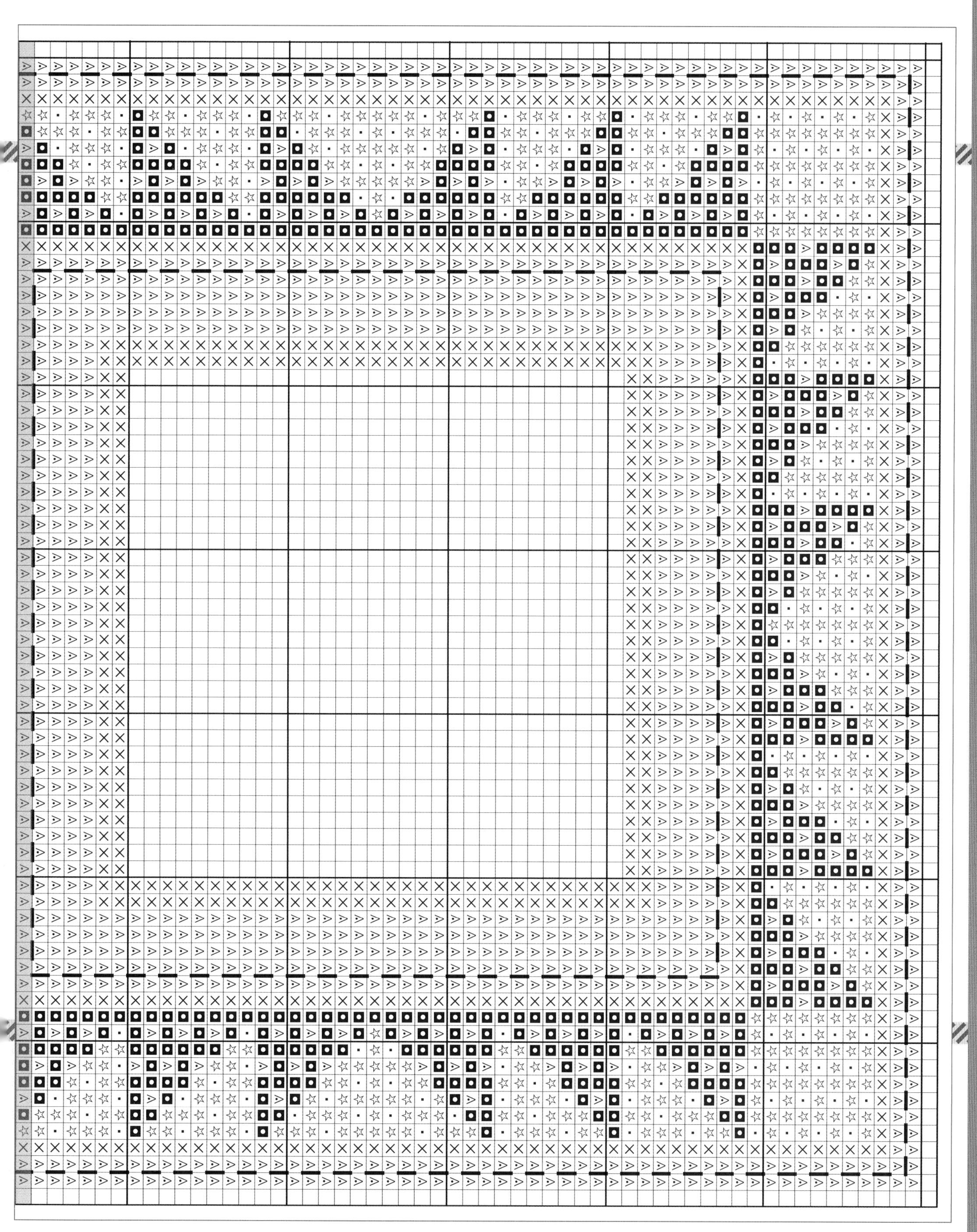

PINEAPPLE INSERT
25 × 25 threads

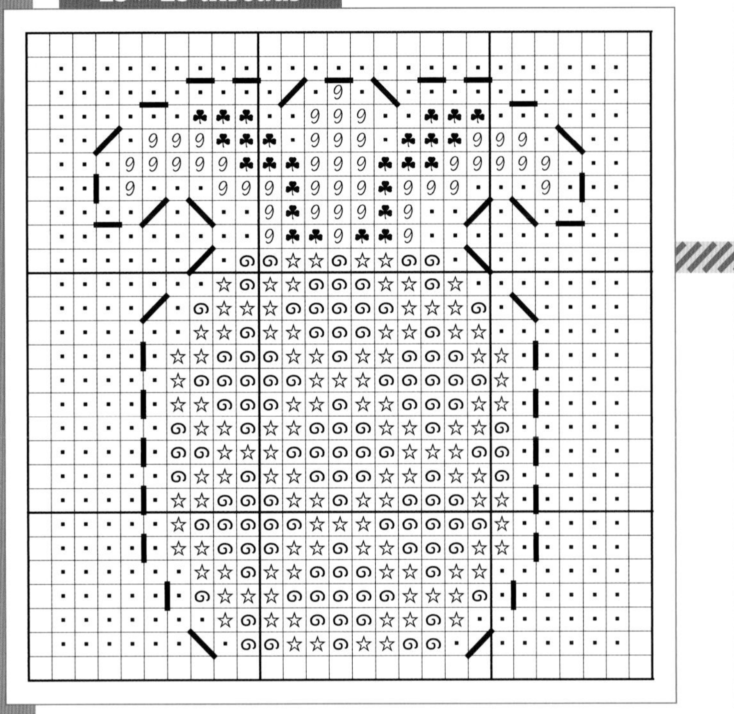

BIRTHDAY CAKE INSERT
25 × 25 threads

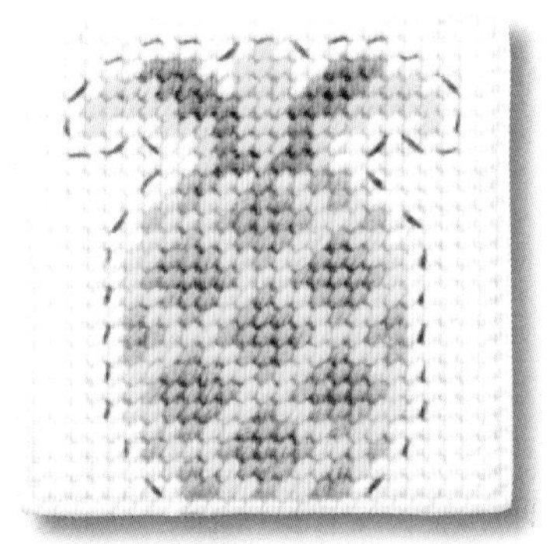

BE MINE INSERT
25 × 25 threads

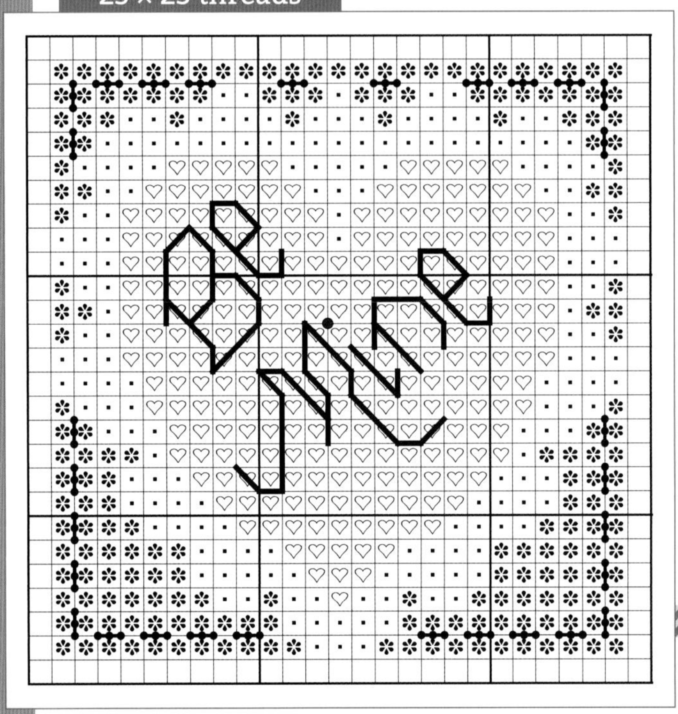

SHAMROCK INSERT
25 × 25 threads

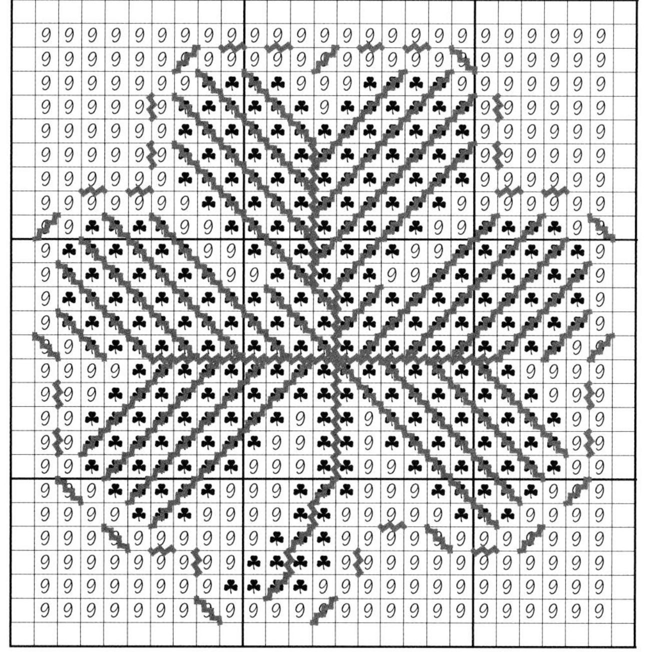

COLOR KEY: PINEAPPLE, CAKE, BE MINE, SHAMROCK, AND EASTER BASKET INSERTS

☆	Bright Yellow
–	Cream
✲	Dark Red
ɷ	Gold
×	Lavender
∀	Light Blue
◎	Light Pink
9	Lime Green
♣	Medium Green
♡	Rose
❀	Rust
▪	White

<u>Backstitch Floss (4 strands)</u>

solid line	Black: dashed lines on pineapple and "Be Mine" on heart
wavy line	Dark Green
dashed line	Medium Yellow
hatched line	Medium Topaz
dotted line	Rose
double line	White

<u>Straight Stitch Floss (4 strands)</u>

solid line	Black: "Be Mine"

<u>French Knot Floss (4 strands)</u>

●	Black: dot on "Be Mine"

Overcast the edges using yarn that matches adjacent stitches.

EASTER BASKET INSERT
25 × 25 threads

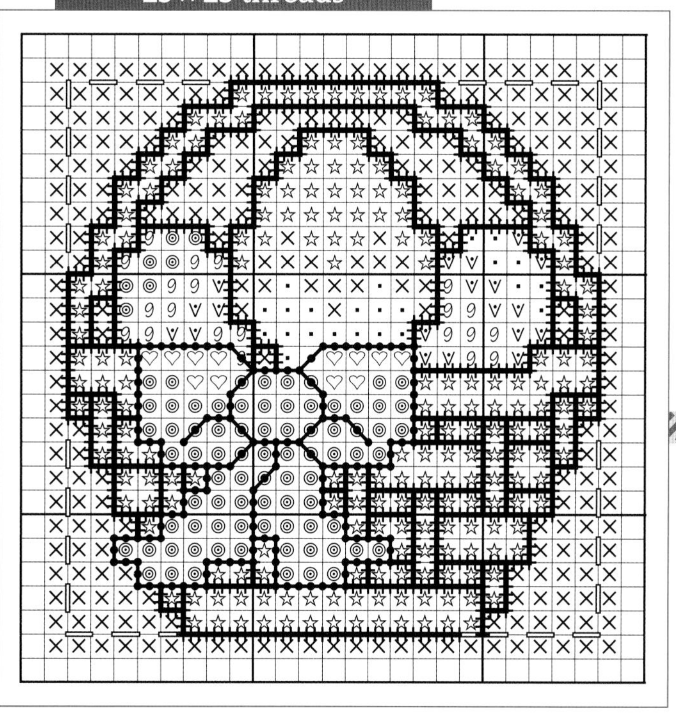

WATERMELON INSERT
25 × 25 threads

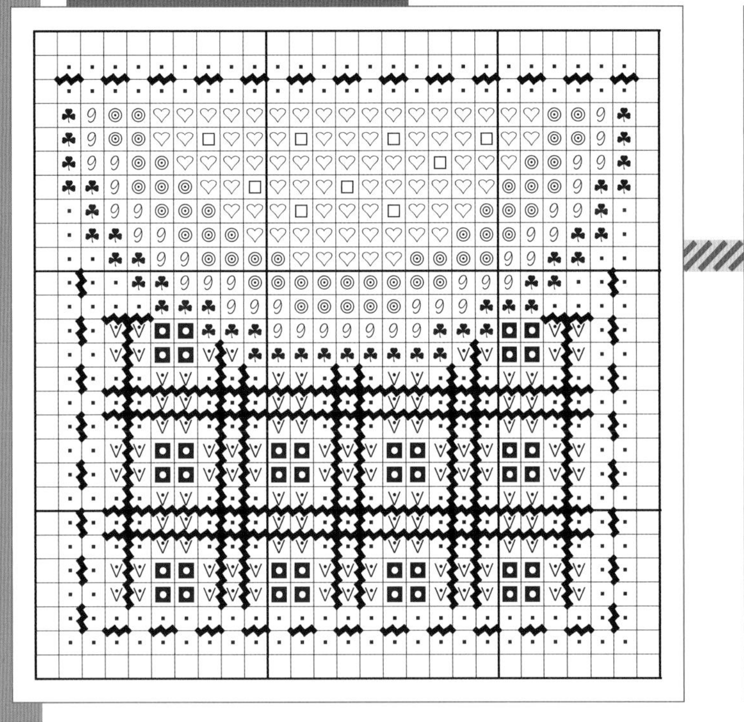

FLAG INSERT
25 × 25 threads

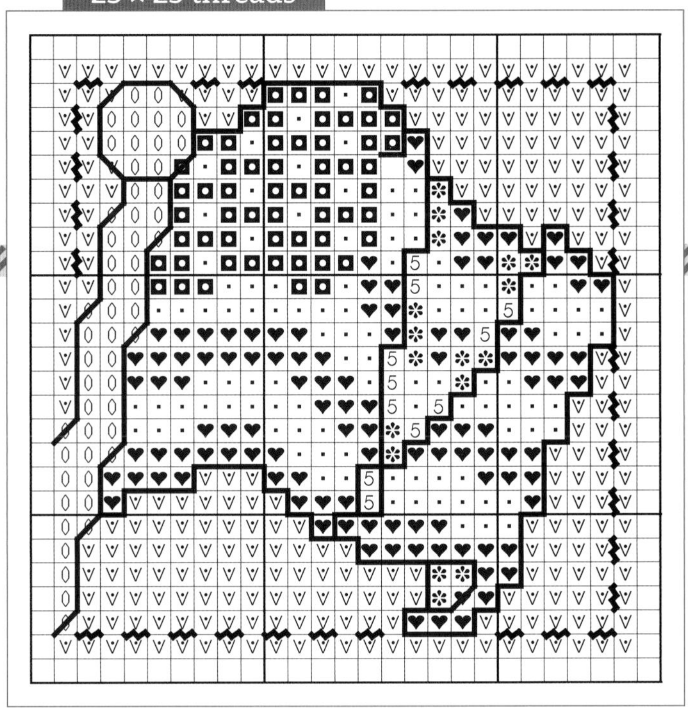

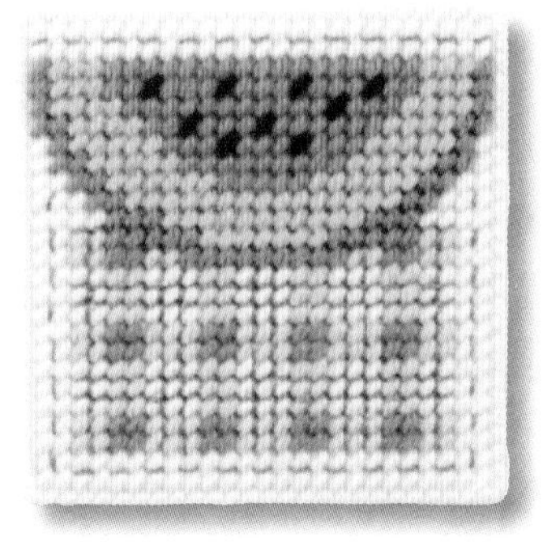

ABC APPLE INSERT
25 × 25 threads

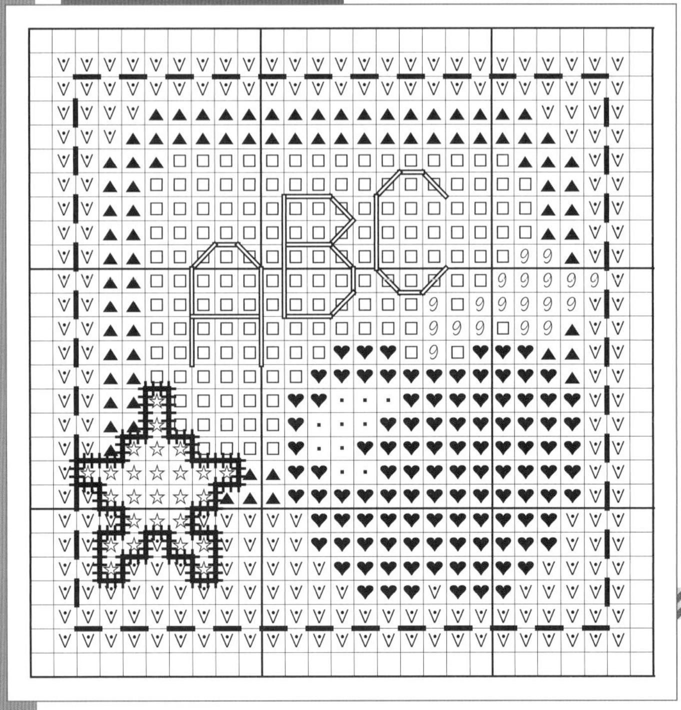

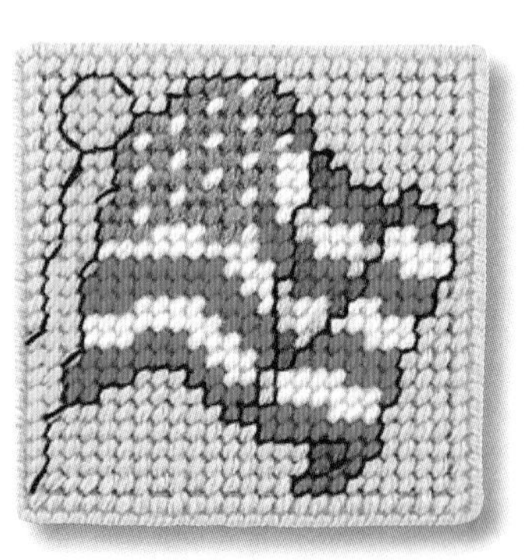

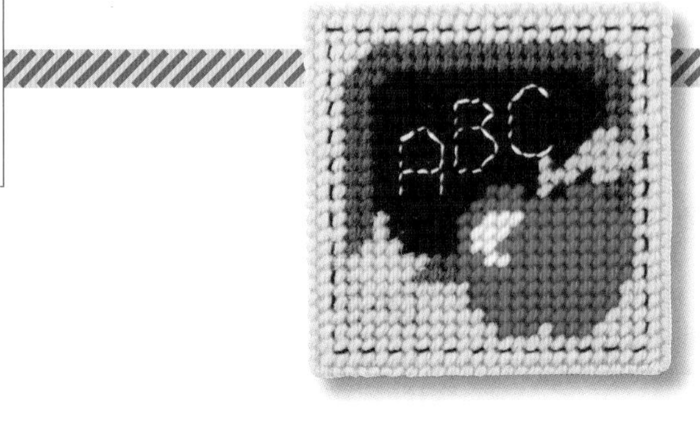

FALL LEAF INSERT
25 × 25 threads

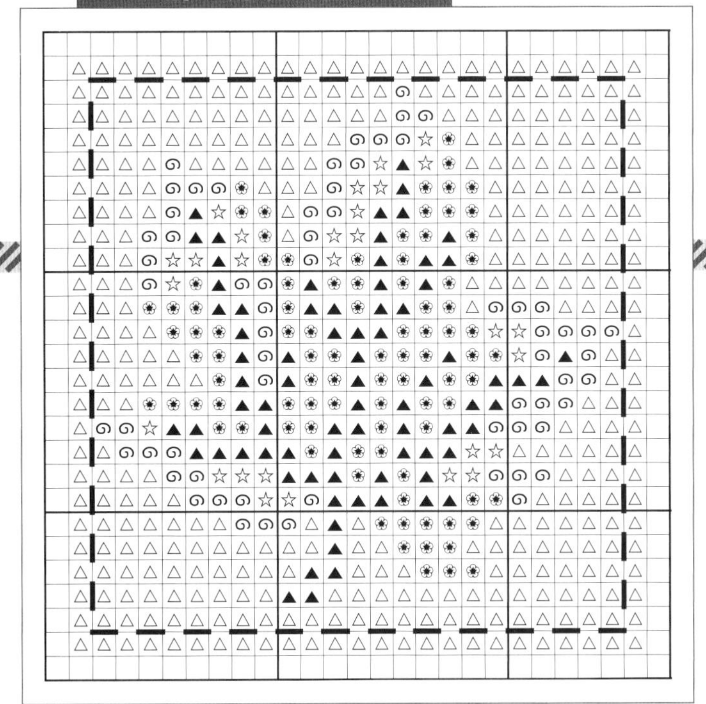

COLOR KEY: WATERMELON, FLAG, ABC APPLE, FALL LEAF, AND PUMPKIN INSERTS

□	Black
☆	Bright Yellow
◘	Dark Blue
✲	Dark Red
ɷ	Gold
V	Light Blue
5	Light Gray
◎	Light Pink
9	Lime Green
▲	Medium Brown
♣	Medium Green
△	Pale Yellow
♥	Red
♡	Rose
❀	Rust
·	White
0	Yellow

Backstitch Floss (4 strands)

———	Black: solid lines on flag and dashed lines around school slate and pumpkin
~~	Dark Blue
———	Dark Brown: dashed lines around leaf and solid lines on pumpkin
++++	Medium Topaz
═══	White

Overcast the edges using yarn that matches adjacent stitches.

PUMPKIN INSERT
25 × 25 threads

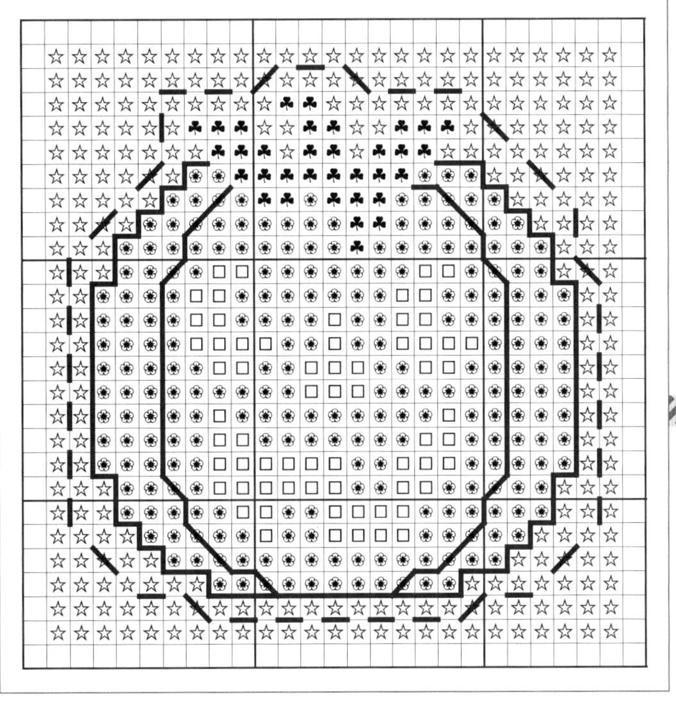

TURKEY INSERT
25 × 25 threads

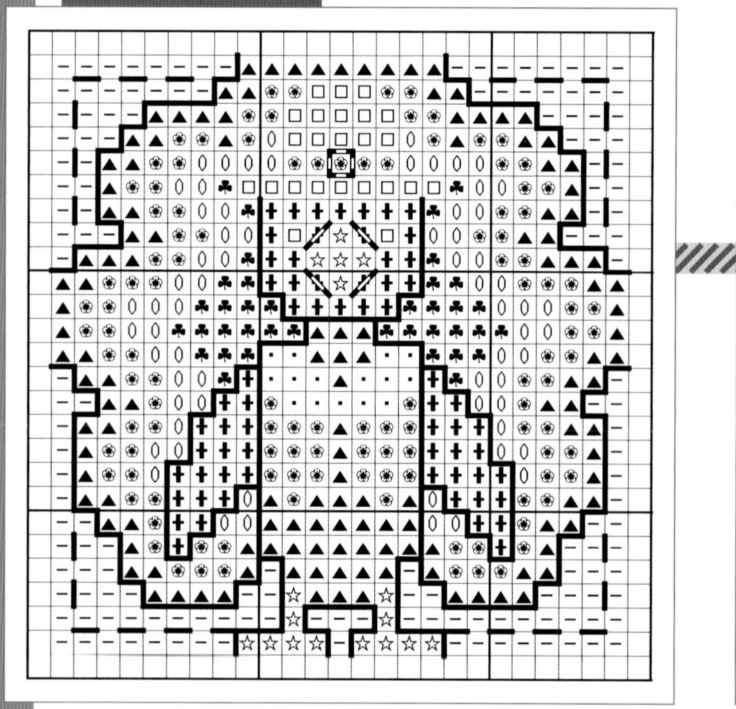

SNOWFLAKE INSERT
25 × 25 threads

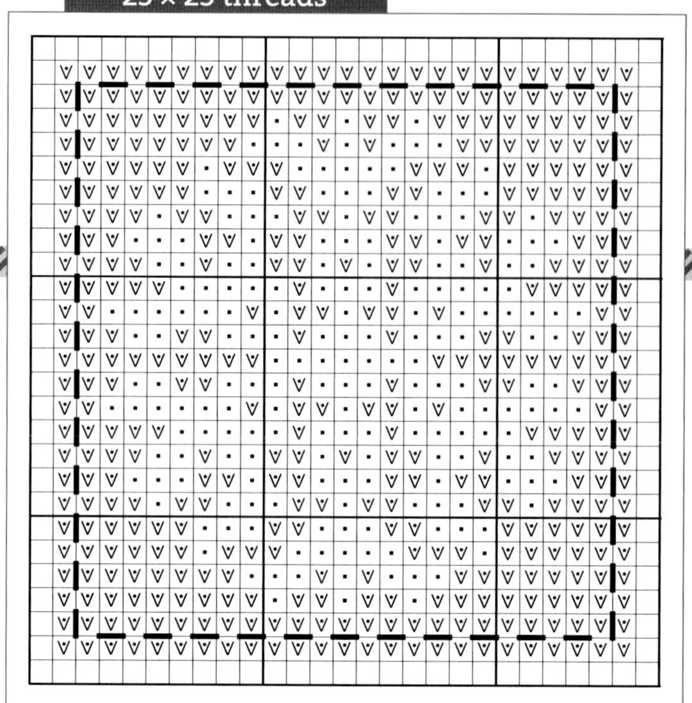

CHRISTMAS TREE INSERT
25 × 25 threads

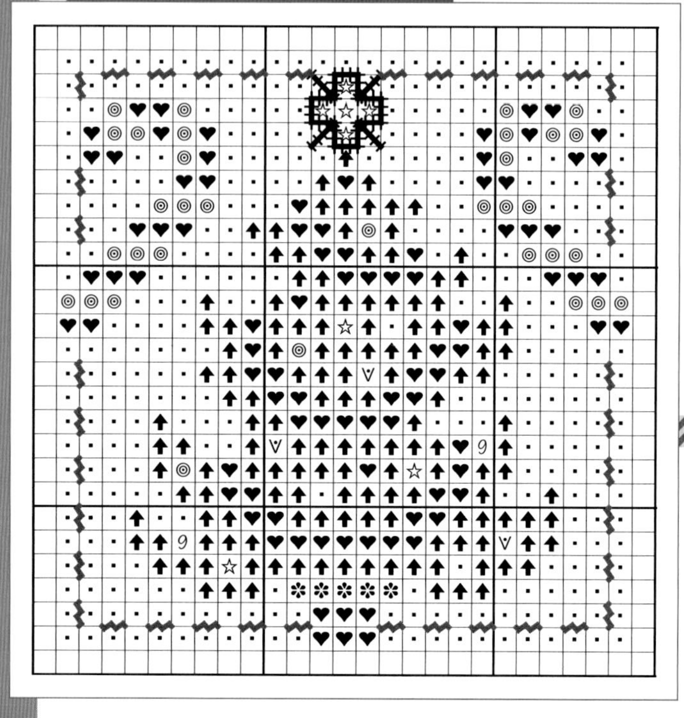

COLOR KEY: TURKEY, SNOWFLAKE, AND CHRISTMAS TREE INSERTS

□	Black
☆	Bright Yellow
–	Cream
✲	Dark Red
⬆	Green
∀	Light Blue
✝	Light Brown
◎	Light Pink
9	Lime Green
▲	Medium Brown
♣	Medium Green
♥	Red
❀	Rust
▪	White
0	Yellow

Backstitch Floss (4 strands)

———	Black: dashed lines around snowflake
———	Dark Brown: dashed lines around turkey and backstitch on turkey
~~	Dark Green
–·–·–	Medium Yellow
++++	Medium Topaz

Overcast the edges using yarn that matches adjacent stitches.

WELCOME TO OUR HOME

INVITE GUESTS into your home with this charming design! Featuring floral and harvest motifs, you'll be able to warmly welcome friends and family when displaying this wall hanging.

WELCOME TO OUR HOME WREATH
79 × 95 threads

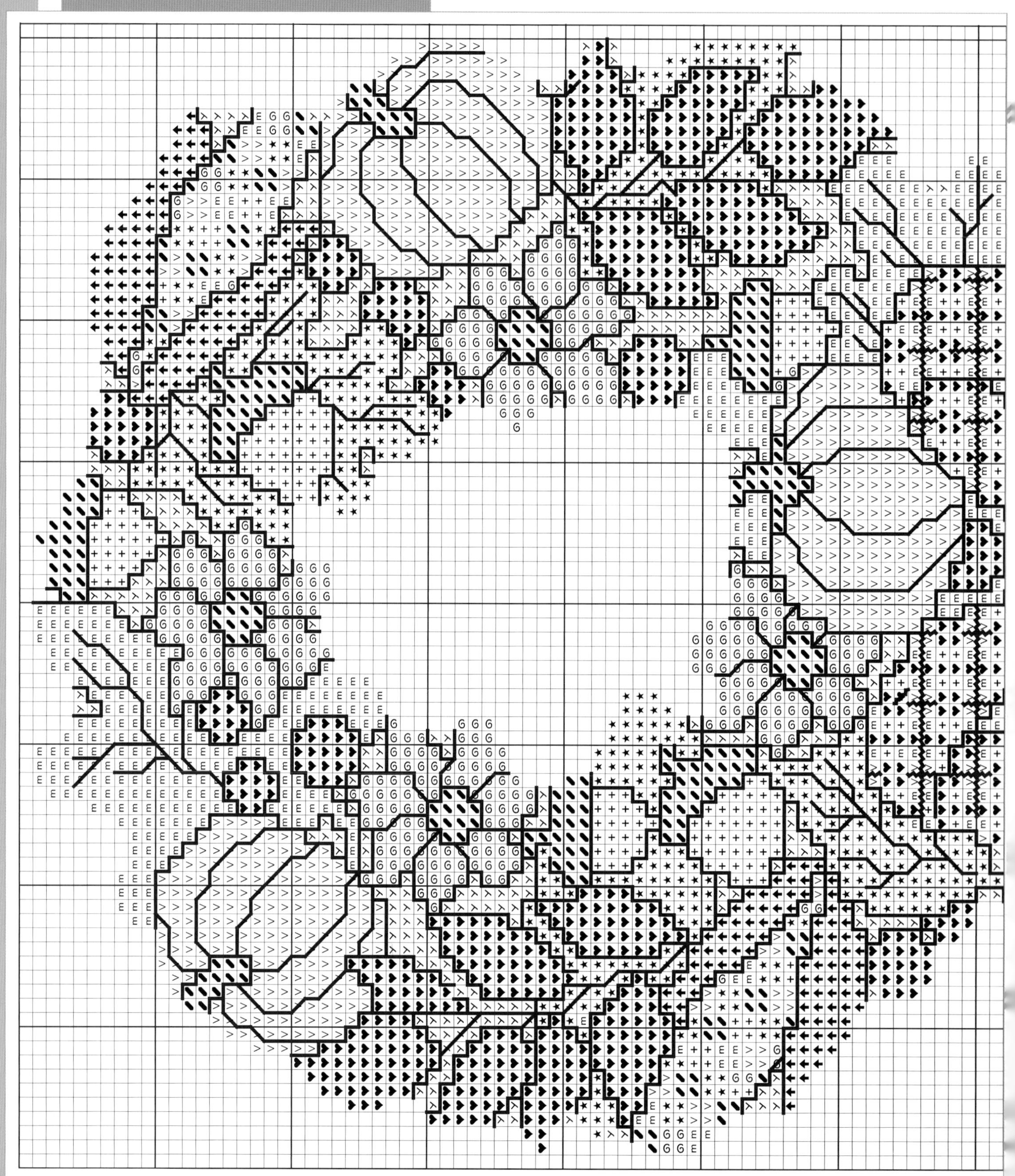

Plastic Canvas Size Needed: 13½" × 16"

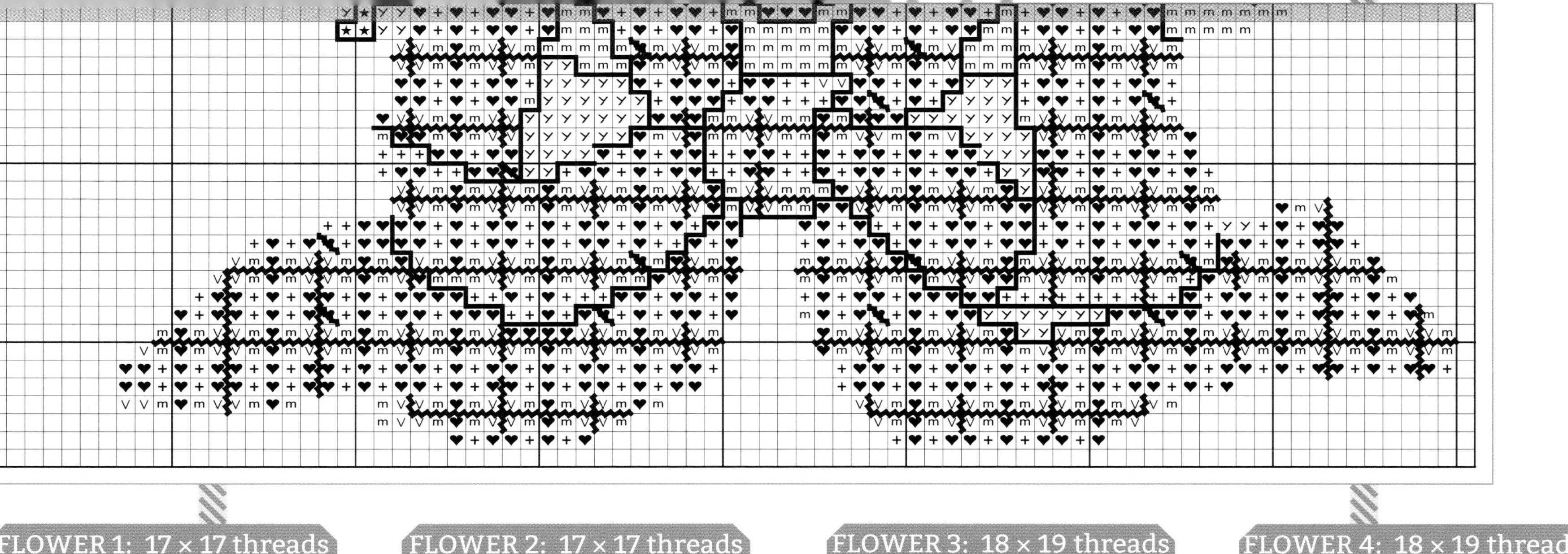

FLOWER 1: 17 × 17 threads

FLOWER 2: 17 × 17 threads

FLOWER 3: 18 × 19 threads (Stitch 2)

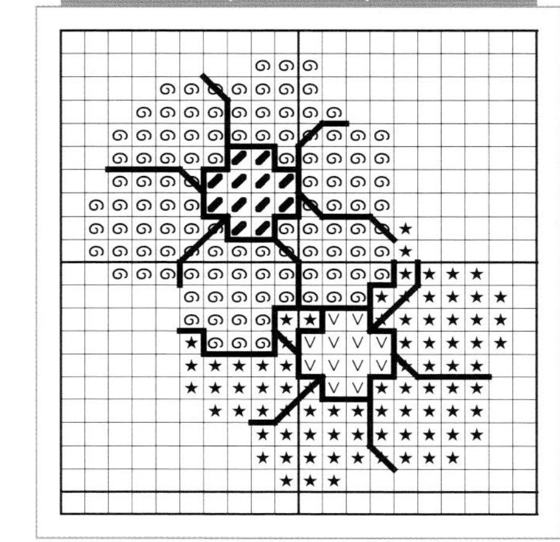

FLOWER 4: 18 × 19 threads

COLOR KEY: WELCOME TO OUR HOME WREATH AND FLOWERS

★	Bright Yellow
❤	Dark Red
ɢ	Gold
+	Light Brown
⁄	Medium Brown
⋎	Pale Yellow
v	Rust
▲	Tan
m	Yellow

Backstitch Floss (4 strands)

———	Black Brown
~~	Medium Garnet

Overcast the edges using yarn that matches adjacent stitches.

▢ Gray area indicates last row of previous section of design.

After all pieces have been stitched, assemble the wall hanging with hot glue, using the flowers to attach the wreath to the signs (refer to the photo for placement).

WELCOME SIGN: 87 × 26 threads

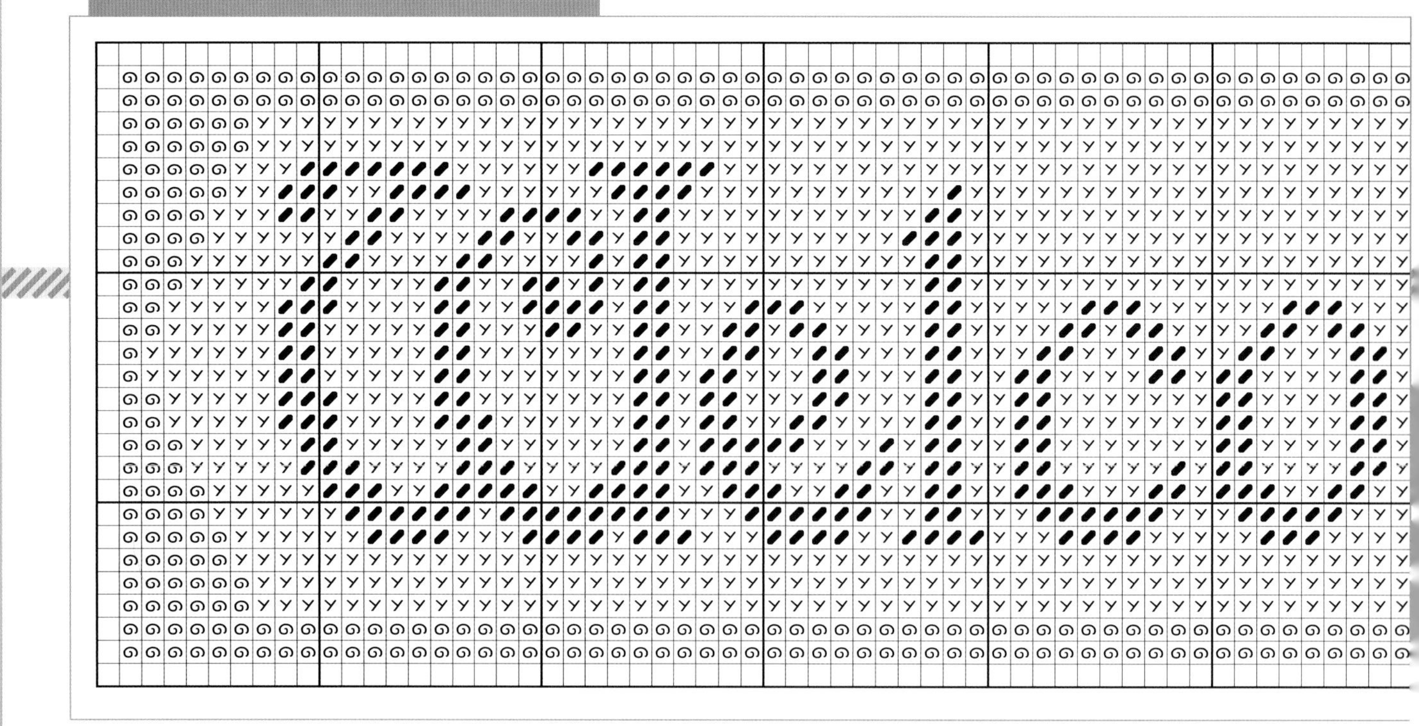

TO OUR HOME SIGN: 87 × 38 threads

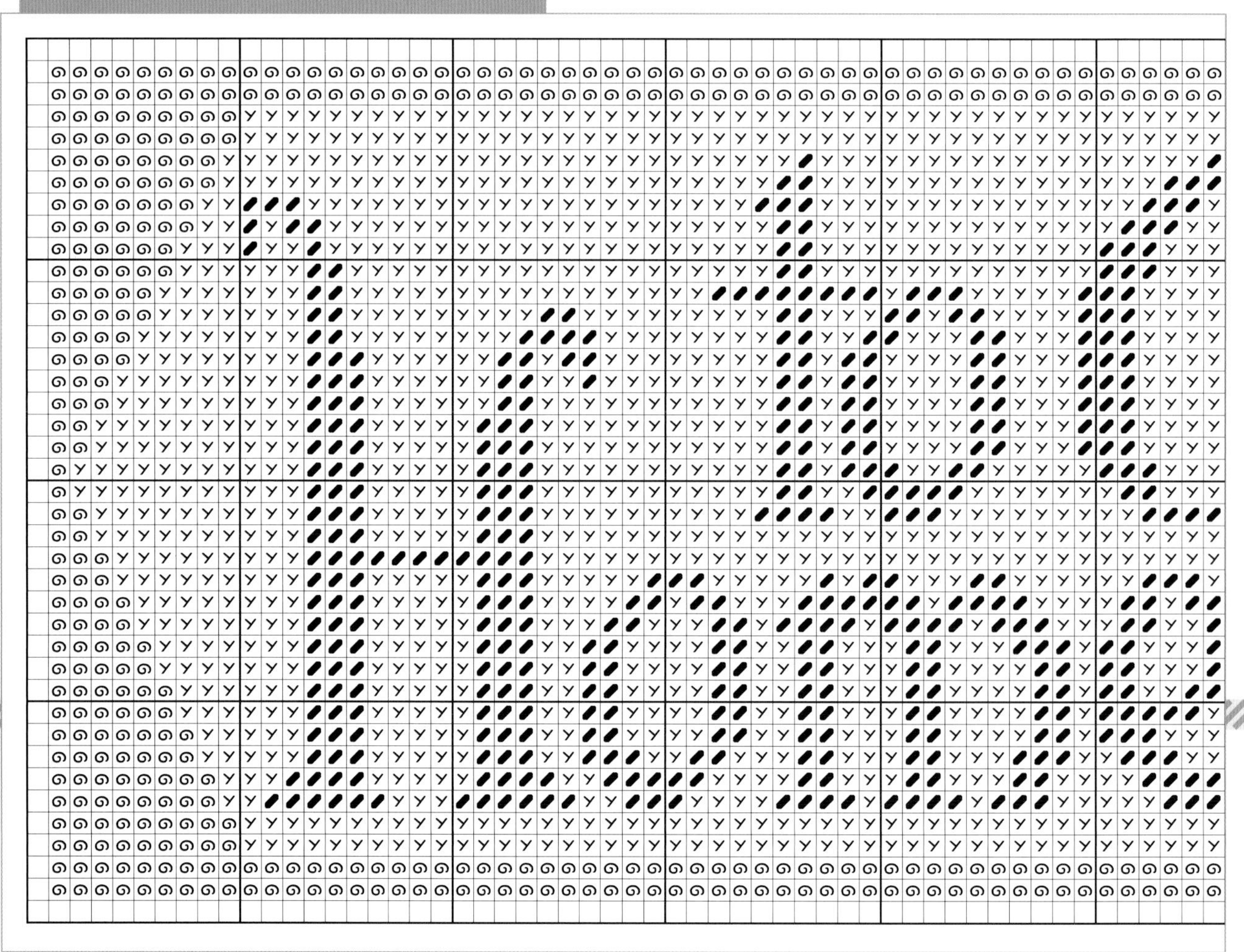

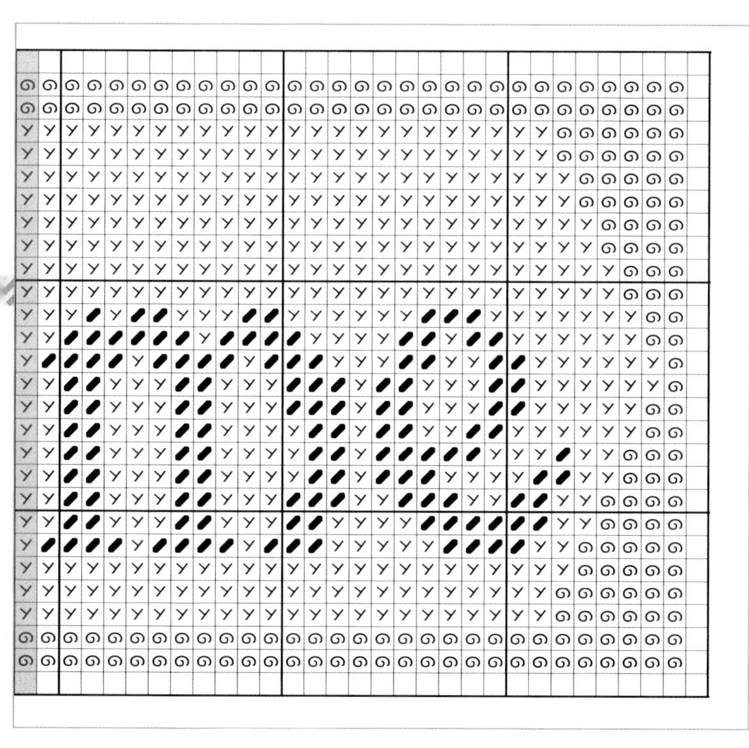

Plastic Canvas Size Needed: 15" × 5¾"

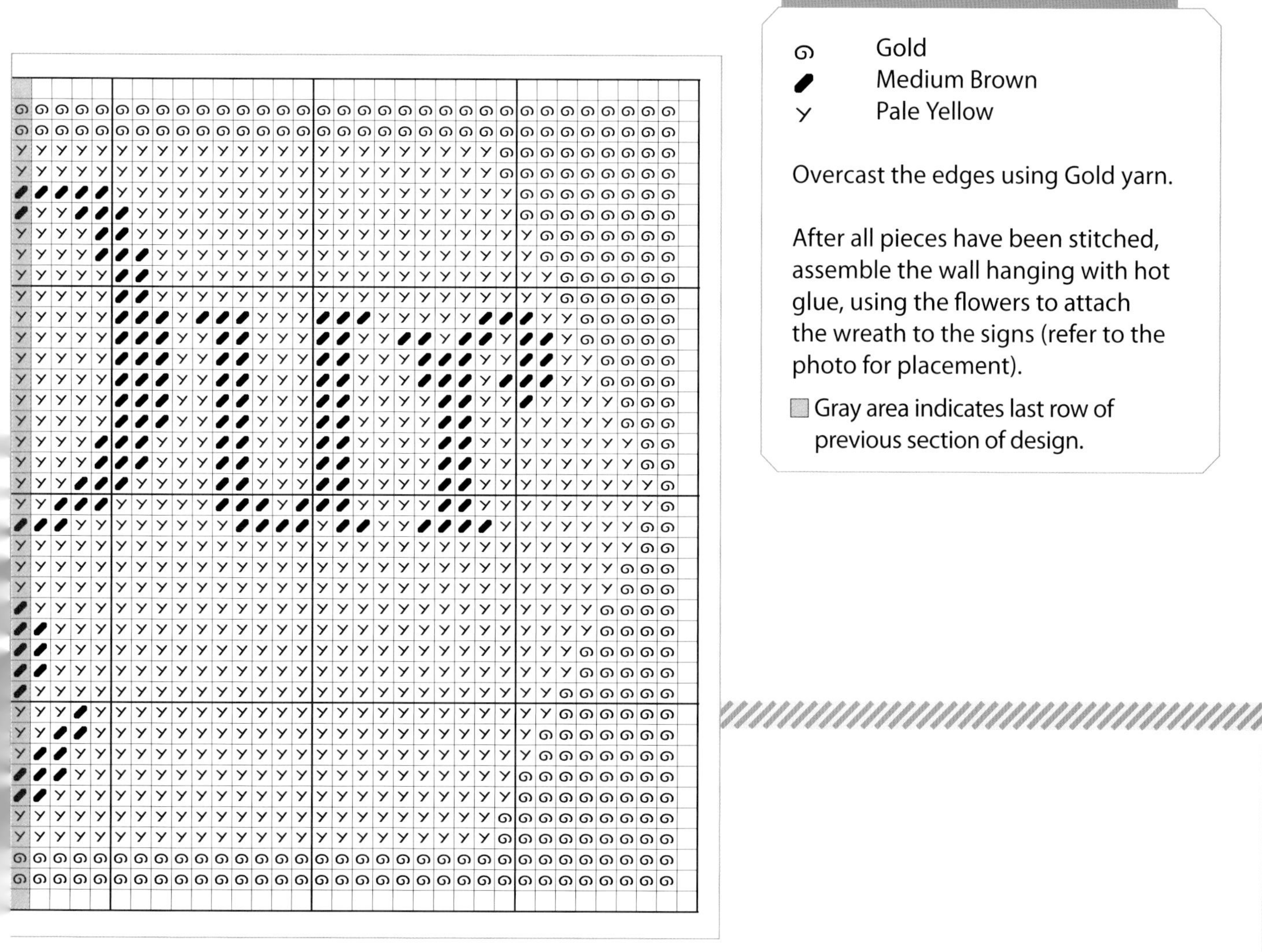

Plastic Canvas Size Needed: 15" × 8"

COLOR KEY: WELCOME TO OUR HOME SIGNS

ᘓ	Gold
⬮	Medium Brown
Y	Pale Yellow

Overcast the edges using Gold yarn.

After all pieces have been stitched, assemble the wall hanging with hot glue, using the flowers to attach the wreath to the signs (refer to the photo for placement).

Gray area indicates last row of previous section of design.

GENERAL INSTRUCTIONS

QUICK TIPS

1. Prior to beginning a project, look over the requirements and directions carefully.
2. Stitch the design on an uncut piece of plastic canvas to avoid snagging yarn or floss on ragged edges. If necessary, cover the edge with masking tape to avoid snags.
3. Some designs require a piece of plastic canvas larger than the standard 10½" x 13½" size. Consult the larger designs for the size of plastic canvas needed and stitch on a piece that accommodates the design size (the smaller designs will fit on a standard sheet of plastic canvas). The designs can also be stitched on two smaller pieces of plastic canvas that equal the required size when joined. Start stitching the top of the design at the top of the first piece of plastic canvas. When you get to the bottom of the first piece, line up the second piece of plastic canvas and use a half cross-stitch to continue the next row in the design (see diagram). As you stitch, make sure the holes in both pieces of plastic canvas line up correctly.

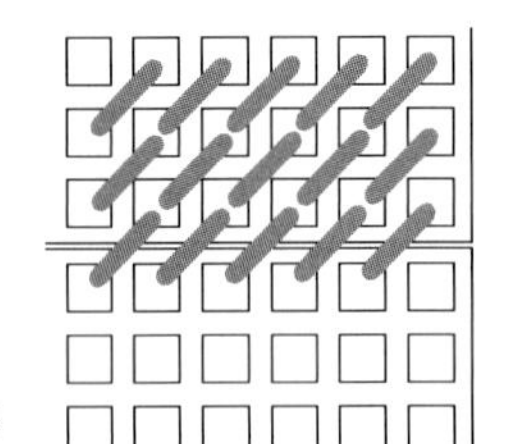

4. For a finished look, trim rough edges and cut off corners at an angle.
5. All pieces are stitched on 7-mesh plastic canvas using a size 16 tapestry needle and worsted weight yarn. Floss details use 4 strands of cotton embroidery floss.

STARTING TO STITCH

All stitches begin on the back of your work. With a threaded needle, come up from the back of your work, hold a 1" section of the yarn against the back of the canvas and stitch over the 1" section. This will eliminate the need for a knot on the end of your yarn and will keep the back side of your work clean and flat. To finish off a color, run the needle under 4 or 5 stitches on the back and clip off. The tension of the stitches will hold the yarn in place and knots will not be necessary.

DIRECTIONS

- Stitch the piece(s). Except where otherwise indicated, ½ cross-stitch is used for all main areas.
- To work the charts, start with the top left stitch using the yarn color indicated on the chart and color key. Bring the needle up from the back of the work at the symbol indicated to create the first stitch (see diagram).
- Cut away surplus canvas. Cut outside and trim the rough edges next to unworked edges. Overcast all edges with matching adjacent color.

CUTTING YOUR CANVAS

Always cut your canvas between the bars, making sure to leave one plastic bar between the stitches and cutting line. By cutting between the bars, you will be assured an adequate amount of plastic for overcasting the edges when finishing (see diagram).

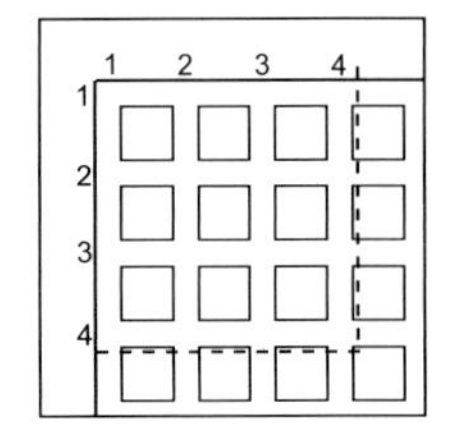

ASSEMBLY

Welcome Home Assembly

After overcasting the edges, back each piece with felt. Cut the felt slightly smaller than the trimmed plastic canvas project. Secure with felt glue or hot glue. Use ribbon to tie a seasonal welcome banner to the house. Tie the ribbon in a bow so you can easily change the signs for the season.

Seasons of Welcome Assembly

After overcasting the edges, back each piece with felt. Cut the felt slightly smaller than the trimmed plastic canvas project. Secure with felt glue or hot glue. Sew metal rings in place on the back of the wall hanging (refer to photo for placement). Cut twenty-six 1" chenille stems. Sew two chenille stems to the back of each mini sign, lining them up with the metal rings on the welcome sign. Bend the chenille stem ends to create hooks, making it easy to change out the mini signs each season.

CLEANING

Hand-wash plastic canvas projects in warm water with a mild soap. Do not rub or scrub stitches, as this will cause the yarn to fuzz. Do not put your stitched piece in the dryer; allow to air dry.

STITCH GUIDE

½ Cross-Stitch

Most commonly used, it is either stitched in rows or columns. This stitch slants up from left to right. Always bring the needle up on odd numbers and down on even numbers.

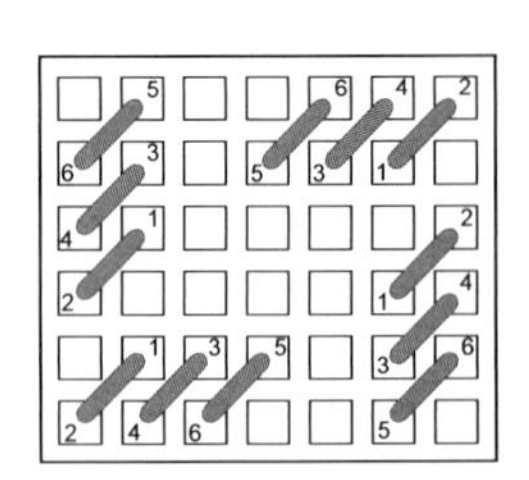

Overcast and Joining Stitch

This stitch is used for finishing your edges or joining two pieces of canvas. The stitch comes up in one hole, over the border bar and up the next hole, over the border bar and up the next hole. For joining, make sure the holes and edges are aligned before stitching.

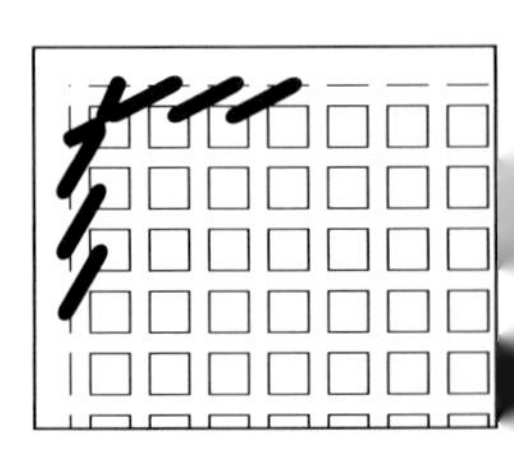

Backstitch

A backstitch is made in any direction with multiple continuous stitches crossing one bar at a time.

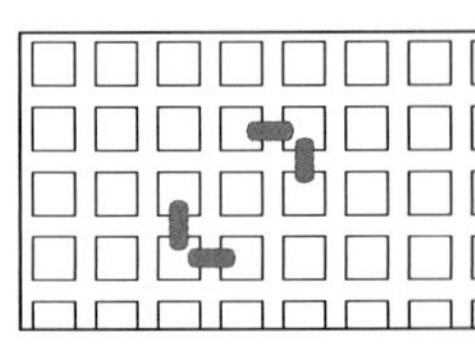

Straight Stitch

A straight stitch is formed by bringing the needle up at 1 and down at 2. The stitch can be of any length and worked in any direction.

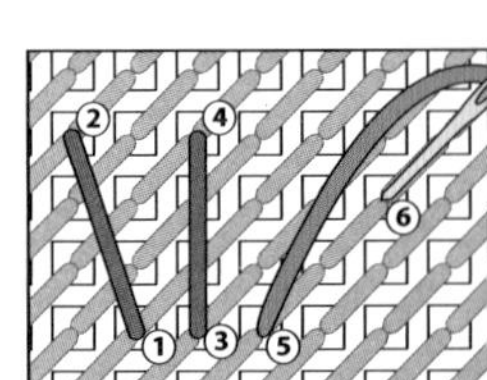

French Knot

Bring the threaded needle through the canvas and wrap the floss around the needle as shown. Tighten the twists and return the needle through the canvas at the same place. The floss will slide through the wrapped thread to make the knot.

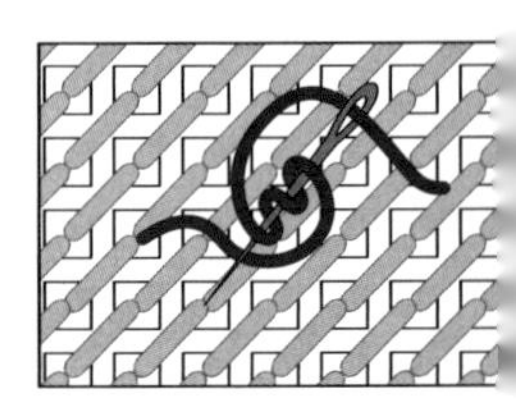

Produced by Herrschners, Inc., for distribution exclusively by Leisure Arts, Inc., 104 Champs Blvd., STE 100, Maumelle, AR 72113-6738, leisurearts.com.

Copyright © 2014 by Herrschners, Inc. All rights reserved. This publication is protected under federal copyright laws. Reproduction of this publication or any other Leisure Arts publication, including publications which are out of print, is prohibited unless specifically authorized. This includes, but is not limited to, any form of reproduction or distribution on or through the Internet, including posting, scanning, or e-mail transmission.

We have made every effort to ensure that these instructions are accurate and complete. We cannot, however, be responsible for human error, typographical mistakes, or variations in individual work.